# THE BODIES

## AND OTHER POLITICAL POEMS

# The Bodies

## and other political poems

Calvin White

NON CANADA

*Publisher's note: This book is a work of fiction. Names, characters, places and incidents are either the product of the author's imagination or are used fictitiously, and any resemblance to actual persons living or dead is entirely coincidental.*

**Library and Archives Canada Cataloguing in Publication**

White, Calvin, 1950–, author
The bodies : and other political poems / Calvin White.

ISBN 978-1-926942-78-0 (pbk.)

I. Title.

PS8595.H4165B64 2015 C811'.6 C2014-908030-1

Printed and bound in Canada on 100% recycled paper.

**Now Or Never Publishing**
#313, 1255 Seymour Street
Vancouver, British Columbia
Canada V6B 0H1

**nonpublishing.com**
*Fighting Words.*

We acknowledge the support of the Canada Council for the Arts and the British Columbia Arts Council for our publishing program.

*This book is for Ziyba.*

*And in memory of Nick Watkins,*
*the epitome of principle, civility, humor, and kind intellect.*

## I Was Washing in the Morning When I Heard

*fuck them all*
that's what Keith said before he drove his car in reverse
up and down Paramount street
Hoover's bakery steaming out the mothering scents of cinnamon
but not for him
his glowing eyes tight curly hair
the cops looking for his guns
his marksman eyes
thin as wheat in the field and shoulders hunched
pitch forking carp in the marsh creek
a quiet beer
alone
the sun sitting atop his squashed home sweat oozing up from the
dry furrows enveloping him like lice
and
later
alone
again
in the locked hospital doors
medication slowing his paces but not the shards in his eyes
and
later
alone
with
his rifle
nuzzled
beneath
his
chin

## Gangsters

gangsters
are real
fingertips with the same cuticles
as the rest of us
rubbing their chin
in the mirror
eyes
that see beauty
bodies that bend for flowers

gangsters
the power
to kill
as many or as few
with
missiles
deadly drones of death
the flicker of an eye
a cocked magnum

strutting about
pompous as loud flatulence
presidents basking in democracy
wine sipping premiers
bearded mullahs
their hands dripping
and tangled
with the same gold jewellery
of a pimp

## Dangerous Sounds

CUNT
TALIBAN
COMMUNIST
CASTRO
NIGGER
TERRORIST
H
O
M
O

hellllo  bayybee . . . . . . . . . this is the BIG BOPPER
my fellow Americans
our nation
is
at
war

Barry Bonds used steroids
Babe Ruth is dead

Oprah spelled backwards is whatplanetareweon

and last but not least

OH          BA                    MA

## 4YEO . . . FYI . . . L8R

I know our young
don't read
words replaced by speed
language by pecks from fingers

a pity
to be so alone
while havoc cleaves

their vibrant eyes
aching for more
but
seeing only the hard glint of superficiality

our young
as lost as stamps
cancelled on long ago letters

what have we done
wilful and vain
what have we done

## In the Years to Come

in the years to come they say we will be
able to talk to our friends on other continents
with a tiny chip in our forehead as we chatter
into the air not a soul around sidewalks not even
noticing the grey cement having seen it all
GPS will be in the same chip just a sharp notion
of when to turn of when to slow down and when
we have arrived no need for a voice unless we
only have the basic plan that movement will consist
of a legion of fitness clubs offering mind exercises
that send the right signals to get the right body
muscles for the right mate or encounter of our choice
that sex will be quite a bit more convenient
not exactly jacking off or jilling off because there
will be no need for hands ha ha look ma no hands
seriously it will only take the mental image of the person
and the desired body part and ooohhhh doesn't
that orgasm feel great feel great feel great feel great
in the years to come they say that there won't be enough
food for everyone but for some of us it will be
more organic and more succulently prepared
microwaves having been scrapped along with
all the cell phones for causing night blindness
and an array of eaten pockspots in the frontal cortex
that sports however won't change the cups still revered
the rings still what drives us the face painting
with team logos only shifting mid-season to
accommodate the marketing necessity of the
mid-season logo change-over because the
front offices have listened to the voices of the fans
who want more pleasure for their hard earned
dollars and the same old logo can get you know
a bit boring a bit yesterday though thrice a season
it's still a rush to do the retro bit with logos of old

and that politicians thank god will no longer be real
people but ideas like a shimmering almost mucousy
mass a hovering phantasmagoria that can be seen
over Mt. Rushmore on clear days or above Buckingham
Palace on cloudy days that turn extra bright
and emit loud barking-like sounds whenever
government bureaucracies screw up or a judge
falls asleep while deliberating on the death penalty
there will still be a death penalty because
well we still have to keep the streets safe
because despite all the advances you can never
really be sure about your neighbor or the revolutionaries
that in the years to come we will be able to laugh
out loud whenever we want without the need
of a joke or pratfall or aha I gotcha moment or
outdoing the asshole next door at the Christmas lights
finally because . . .once again think GPS
that there will be enough oxygen and water since
energy can neither be created nor destroyed
and pills can be made for every need though some
may not be able to afford them but the law of supply
and demand and the capacity of every human being to
achieve their goals if they are willing to work
hard enough will salve any guilt because after all
if accountability gets taken out of the equation
then we're all screwed and God will still be here
speaking in more tongues than ever because
with all that progress growth and modernity
has given us it is essential for us to remember
our place that without God's grace we would not
have daily bread and even Buddhists will believe
in God because He's real and all in all life is what we
make it and most of us chose ours before we were born

so in the years to come in spite of what they
say all I'm really hoping for
though I can't say counting on
is that the basic premise is accurate
that there actually are years to come

## A Purring Sound

I sit at my desk watching them
all these different shapes chewing up their time
they are the grade eights
*I'm thirteen* one boy said to me this afternoon
at the dance performance
and later demonstrated to the whole class
how when the pretty female dancer jumped
and spread her legs far apart her crotch made a purring sound
I am the substitute
now called the teacher on call
like the janitor is now the custodian
it was my duty to respond responsibly to that crudity
we went outside the classroom to sit on a hall bench
the glass in the door window reverberated from the pandemo-
nium at my leaving the others unsupervised
the boy sat calmly beside me
I asked about his family
then why he had put on that crude show
he said it just blurted out
I said he was doing it to get attention
that it was insulting to the girls
he said he just blurted it out

no one in that class liked the dance performance
another young fellow insisted that one of the male dancers was
gay

these kids don't see the world yet
they just know their world
its gadgets
and ease
its sex
and missing fathers
its noise
and the silence in their homes

## Single

single
each of us born and
die
single
along the way it's another matter because every moment of the
outside
touches
and makes
us
my children are old now and have been without a single parent
from birth
so cluttered
I am a plumber
she is an alcoholic
he is mentally ill
she is lost in affliction
she has been abused
she has been abused
she has been abused
the water in the lake is only frozen in the coldest weeks
we have wind when we need it
and roses
as fragrant as warm hands
bloom
each spring
yes, we live still
apart
but only
on the outside

## Mountain Water

my son faces his palm out toward the pine
the slices of white etching the lake surface beyond our dried grass cliff
*wouldn't it be great if we could hold the wind*

along this ridge are seeds
their whispers swept by silence

we sit together feeling
the bite of the late autumn
the crisp glow of high sun

his palm turns this way and that
waiting

the pine its tufts of spikes waxen
a juniper near our legs

the dried filaments of a fallen dragonfly

if we leave here
we will become again
what we were

but if we wait

## I'm Waiting

I am waiting
as pretentious as it may be

for the young boys to rise up

against the way the world is
its dishonest smiles

to speak their anger
and expectations

to ask for more
not more money or toys
or basketball bling

for the young boys to rise up
and ask the young girls for dates
to bow before them and pray
their forgiveness
ask them to rise up and lead
the song

I'm waiting for that song to begin
for the pine trees to stop dying
and listen to the song
to wonder at its melody

for the young girls to drop their hair
press their thighs and
laugh so loud the crows
go silent
the fish pause in dark pools
and in every jungle the vines

sweat with hope

I'm waiting for that song

I know they can sing
I have seen their mouths open
I have touched their warm fingers
looked deeply into their young eyes
and I know they know
we can do better

what Gandhi spoke
what Ferlinghetti wrote
what Jesus heard
was nothing more than
waves upon a shore
was nothing more than arms around
a mother's neck
that it really is that simple

I'm waiting

for that

and that

and

that

## Love Poems

love poems
hide amongst the reeds
braided and tight
in any water

survival from mounds of Haitian concrete
or in Mickey Mantle's bat
the crack in stadium silence

the way a frightened father
holds his son's hand on the way
to appointments
snug with each other's heartbeat

or asleep the first timers
caress and move throughout
the night as though this was
how it's always been

we say hello
look back upon leaving
drop bread upon the concrete
for mewing cats

say we
or us
nod when miners reach the surface
from far-off
or black tar
is scraped from feathers

the plastic flowers
candle ash
alone
on hillside graves

## For Now

we tell stories to each other
exchange the latest line-up of aphorisms questions taunts
wonderings
espouse our opinions on those we love and those we hate
and look away
if we couldn't do things together
to pass the time
how hard would it be
to breathe in the silence

that comes
from not knowing how to be

but thank god He gave us the internet

the Buddhists call it *maya*
our perception of existence
illusion
*cyber maya*
friendship with the keys at our fingertips
lightning speed
voiceless
communication
our hieroglyphics

for now
we have forests
the steady sound of water flowing
rivers taking us far into ourselves
for now
we have butterflies emerging from crawling creatures
no one knows why
salmon that smell the spirit of rocks
where they were born

and our own beating hearts
waiting to be touched

## Dans une Maison sur L'avenue Casgrain

my son lives in Montreal
he studies French
works in a call centre
walks home alone
on the sidewalk of Avenue Casgrain
just off Rue Ste.Viatour'

he dreams music
violins
the shallow waters of Moberly Lake
their small smooth stones
beneath his bare summer feet
three thousand miles from
the call centre

he is a Cree
smudges with the elders
and their violins
still makes small fires by the St. Lawrence
the Lachine
growling beneath the bobbing mergansers

ta'nsi keeya
he answers

each crackle of his small fire
fidgets with the river air
the coming October cold
my son rubs his hands together

## From the Chipped Blue Cup

of course she is dying
the air pushing in and out of her lungs
hard and riddled
her skin is tight to the cheek
smile brighter than agony
we all know her name
the form she lies upon
the same straight lines

but look
her fingernails still being painted
with tiny flowers
tea steam still puffing
from the chipped blue cup

she sees the white mountains
far in the distance
the dark trees
lacing rocky slopes
and wonders of the winds
they face

## Slaughter

walking along a seawall on any coast
and the gulls crafting the blue
there is only that moment
tongues of song crashing the rock
from a billion years
the same
and who do we think we are

clearing the bodies of great trees
sleeping children
as though
it has no meaning
the rise and ebb of child chest tides
Assad Bush Obama Osama Putin al-Bashir Netanyahu
the boogie-man rhyme

Walmart Shell Pepsi Cola diamond mine golf tournaments
cut it down for Brazil and sell it for value added
the dead fish and dead dead
have all the money in the world
to blow on you and me

wear that suit as straight as ice
between the aisles of dignity
and breathe
breathe who we think we are

that little boy with the itchy elbow and rubbing at his nose
staring at now
hasn't got a chance

does he

## India

I take kids to India
so they can see truth
walking in leper sores
while I squeeze their tiny fingers until
an orange drops into the palm
make them take it back remove the peeling
so that mouth can eat

the fibered legs pushing pedals
to take them wherever they want
as they watch the sweated back before them flow and surge
these school kids from here
as close as a kiss
not even knowing
the fellow's name

so they can sit on stones at night
in the warm air of intimacy
whispering
as street dogs move nearby
and glass bangles tinkle in their sleep
as the body fires glow
smoke sifting upwards
to the same stars

## The Sweet

persimmons
orange eyes
stickiness
the shadings of political language
not at all like persimmons
holding
hidden hostages
us
we don't even realize it
we just buy and buy
the sweet buy and buy
a rapper buys machine guns
a star buys women
it's not possible to prevent
dirt from the fingernails
podiums
are for players
and we
we are always
the fans

who's in the hospital
skin loose
eyes watery
voice slow and soft

who no longer remembers when

## Predator

the aboriginal girl stands
eating saskatoons
in the clumps of bushes
edging the parched yellow grass of the school yard

it's July
and the school windows have been boarded over for weeks
to prevent summer damage

she's 12, maybe 13
and all alone

the berries pop nimbly into her mouth
fat and sweet
a slight trace of purple stains her lips

she thinks of nothing but the succulent fruit
hasn't heard the chatter of the two older girls
crossing the school yard metres away
and cussing their boyfriends, calling them *fucking stupid*

hasn't noticed the older man
leaning across the wire fence
farther back on the sidewalk

leaning over and watching

## The Silence of Slices

when a machete slices into your flesh

does it matter whether you're only six
or seventy-six

does the shock of that vicious blade
driving into your flesh
shift to intense pain
immediately

and does the sheer intensity continue
or subside as soon as the next
hack
slices
into a different part of your
body
bringing new excruciation

does the back
register the same magnitude
of pain
as the backs of the legs

is it better
if it's just one machete
striking over and over
rather than several machetes
swinging altogether

once the first slice
draws your full attention
do you see the others

does the flesh part like meat in a shop
with each slice
or does the body
decide to resist
in different places

does a toddler
fully know
what is taking place

does a baby
know at all

and
does the shock
the pain
of the slicing
come with a realization
that death is next

does it ever cross your mind
that no matter
how loudly you scream
no one
seems to hear

## On the Move

I knew a man once who was throwing stones into the sea
one after the other for hours
I didn't know whether he was trying to clear the shore
or fill the ocean
 after 17 years his wife left him
and their three kids
he had always smiled when he told me
*I don't know what she sees in me*
so he drove 900 miles
shot himself in the foot
and drove 900 miles back
 when he came to see me he was limping
staring through me with pale blue hollow eyes
 told me how his wife had fallen in love
with a guy in the next town named Lucky
angular guy with an old black Pontiac
denim jacket and a string tie when he went to the bar
*I'm in love with Lucky* she stated
and that was it
 he asked me for a cup of tea for the road
said he had to keep moving
was on his way
to the ocean

## French Class

the students sit in their klatches of animated chatter
this is group work in French class
group work to develop a document about truth
they need to know all of it by tomorrow
they have been very productive
it is 10:14 in the morning
they see love as deeply meaningful
his arm moves closer to the back of her soft neck
she blushes and her muted giggle is only heard by him
the quiet ones in the corner hold their yellow duotangs
as amulets for the future
Brandon chews mint gum
he says it's to clear his head
these kids want to go with the flow
they muse about real life
wonder where it is
and who has it.

## You Take Me For a Fool

you take me for a fool
when you say you cut yourself
craft images with each slick slice
to bathe away the boredom
with your blood

how it's just the thing
a commitment to be real
a shriek against the wind
and laughter at the game

how feeling's done today to make
a point
edges to find edges
and all art is sacred
that's just the way it is
the way it ought to be

and I look at your scars and cry
only find the words to say
*you've cut yourself*

## Silver Creek

the cows all perched along the side of the green hill
tight to the slope
and nodding
at the grass

this isn't Austria
no valley of the Alps

this is Silver Creek

where horses can starve
and children
get tugged along
by frightened hands
from eruptions in a kitchen

and the raging man in the field

the hay all coiled up around him
in massive round bales

as tight as this evening's
summer heat

## Young Girl on the Step

she came to the door
a basketball in her long fingers
wondering if he was home
would answer

her dark curls
late afternoon leaves falling
the scent of green grass
pulled from the flower bed
bulbs hidden for spring

her fingers tapping the ball

the window
covered in steam

her lips tight
like hopes

## Mason's Daughter

Mason's daughter died
I read the obituary in the paper

her 16 year old smiling face
golden curls
she had moved away
left the missing limbs
of her youth

the rope around her neck
didn't belong to her

nor to Mason

the rough fibres
more intricate than memory
more adhesive
than blood

the rope was in her hand
when she was born

the rough fibres
drawn like shrapnel
beneath her skin

only time
and circumstance
could know how long
her heart
would take to drop away
find a wind
to soar with

## Taliban

Orwell could not have imagined the name
our enemies would be given
the armoured Humvees
black body bags
and blessed shrapnel

but he could have guessed
who would have the most fear
the greater need
for deception

how easy it would be
to suit up words
in freedom
country
sacrifice

how easy it would be
to forget

## At Terezin

at Terezin
they sell tickets for 150 crowns
into the ghetto museum
its fragments of dimming light
the shards of drawing paper

*crows on a wire*
Arnost   age 12

*a dog and cat*
*beneath the kitchen table*
Eva   age 9

reminding us of those moments
when time has no tongue
has not lost its bumblebee wings

the walls of numbered suitcases
dolls stitched to smile
lists of names
the proud performance programs
for basement 6
smoky swirls of limbs and heads
curling in unending queues
orderly to the trains
painted by Fritta
whose brushes knew
what his mind wouldn't allow

the admission
includes entrance to the Small Fortress
a prison since 1786
home to the assassin of Archduke Ferdinand
its muted brick walls
colder than this winter

frozen with whispers about hope
and the empty S.S. swimming pool
cozy movie theatre
echoes of the latest from Berlin
driven still in the oak panels of the stage
the solitary cells
black with ghost prisoners
refusing to leave
forcing us along the underground passage
past the mortuary room
to the execution grounds
canopied platform to keep the marksmen dry
fifty paces from the mound
against the wall
and to the side near the other entry
a scaffold
all in this silent grassy courtyard
just metres from
the mass gravesite
where the bodies were strewn
like twisted branches
from a windstorm

150 crowns
gets you all of this
and more
the cramped basement barracks
filled with bunk beds as tight
as it was in 1943
when the 140,000
were modelling such lively culture
for the Red Cross inspectors
and tucked together with prayers
regularly forming for delousing

but there is no charge
to visit
the crematorium
or the long rows of flat granite
markers huddling straight and silent
in this evening's dropping cushion of fog

## Numbers on Graves at Terezin

#215?
can you hear this laughter?
the load of school boys jostling past you
on tour
this cold winter day
January's snow crusted inches above you
bare thorns to the side
dried withered roses
farther along
what about you #216?
is it cold enough?
and do they have your permission
for a snowball battle
just outside the execution ground
dodging and lunging
gouging up another volley of snow
#217
any reaction?
a comment?
they're lighting up smokes
stamping about underfoot
releasing a glob of spit
as they tease about each others' girlfriends
#218
what do you think?
should they sit in silence
in the S.S. theatre
their backs stiff in the polished
wooden seats
for a short black and white reminder
of the camp
#219?
#220?
#221?

#222?
#223?
#224?
all of you so straight in your row
the same height and length and width
perfect tidy symmetry
like a pretty parade of stillness
polite square footprints of granite
arranged to please the eye

or rows ahead  #775
you have a name
Josef Koubek
and you were born
in December on the 18th
1913   that was a Thursday
likely another cold day
maybe snowing
right around Hanukkah
a nice blessing you must have been
and only 32 years later
you were put here
May 9, 1945  the day after the war ended
the camp doors wide open
green sprigs bursting from every
space in the bricks
the sun so warm to the cheek
in early morning
and your turn came
to take a number

## Zidovske (Jewish) Cemetery, Prague

can I take your name
for this page
your time
how you awoke on dreary mornings
happy to see rain on the window
reached over to the glass
the movement of your body
as you rose from the bed
and at the mirror
saw the aging of your skin

never saw the smooth black marble
gold etching
hidden by a blanket of ivy
six million green leaves
veined and green and always fresh
the great sycamore towers
forever on guard
and row upon row of trails
and markers
whispers circling
flittering in the wind
*and many more*
*. . . . . and many more*

## Public Announcement

on the cold yellow wall just above the top row of seats in Paegas Arena
site of Hockey Club Sparta
its thousands of rabid chanting fans
drums and pompoms thrusting
site of trade fairs
and concerts
the Iron Curtain
would never have permitted
Mötley Crüe
Deep Purple
site even of a talk by
the Dalai Lama
for twenty metres
stretching the full length of the wall
high above the ice
*Andrea, Andrea, Andrea, Andrea, Andrea* . . . . . . . .
each declaration written
in small perfect persistent letters
only the young
feel such love

## Two Czech Artists

Vaclav Chad was twenty-two
when he died
shot by the Nazis
as he tried to run away
his painting oils
all turning to black

it's terrifying
to think of dying
being no more
a set of numbers
in someone's memory
if you're lucky

Jaroslav Cermak
painted the Montegrin lady
when he was forty
and died eight years later
he saw and felt
the stunning softness of her face
the lines from her eyes to chin
how she dipped her wrist
as she spoke

each morning he awoke to newness
leaned over the stone ledge
beneath his window
roundly peering across the square
his hands touching that texture
gripping the fine markings
from a workman's chisel
and cried out to friends
a cousin carrying fresh bread

a young man walking Russian wolfhounds
in the rain
drops splashing from their soggy fur

did he wonder how much longer he'd live
would eight years have seemed a fortune
or a curse
how much is time worth
names
saying every name you've heard
to prove you really were
pleading to hear your own voice once more
not have it seen on etched marble
above a date of start and end
waiting for Sunday visitors
that forever pass it by
your photos flat and worn
who was that again?

how much is time worth
the stroke of each brush
slightly more patient
colour just right
a bluer blue
the green of branches
finding a scent of spruce
gaze becoming arm
hand becoming brush
and you are the paint
texture spread to last forever

## Celebration

on this 14th century bridge
black granite faces of saints
overseeing the daily throngs of tourists
some gypsies have gathered
to throw flowers into the water
the spring torrent of the Vltava
yellow daffodils
their bright mouths announcing
the visit of another year
of gypsy existence

some gypsies
only a handful
arriving from wherever
and TV cameras
reporters to catch the moment
the proof of gypsy progress

then a trio of small children appear
ushered forth in traditional costumes
maybe three, five, and six years old
two boys and a girl
as vulnerable as the daffodils
to the force of a hand
or a brick
all alone in the centre of Charles Bridge
the photographers squatting
inches from their charming innocence
the youngest with a cough
while several metres away
to both sides
watch the black uniformed state police
riot clubs hanging ready
just in case the skinheads arrive

## Roma of Zabijanec

Zabijanec    as in Zah Bee Yaneetz
from the root word zabit
to kill
this outdoor cave of decay
a mini Dresden with tin patched roofs
eight or more to a room
hundreds of humanity
limping and festering and laughing
tugging at me        *uyoh!*
*uyoh!*    *uyoh!*
but I am not their uncle
and my photographs bring no blessing
nor pittance of succour
my photographs
steal moments of flesh
glimpses of eyes from windows
in these iron factory hovels
forty years of eyes
and ladders rising to the second story
perches for these ravens
staring at me in smouldering doubt
*uyoh!*
*uyoh!*
their one water tap
their old men with walking sticks
their infants fleeing in terror
from the white voyeur
infants suckling at a breast
coloured washing limp in the sun
the concrete ruins that front this bombed out complex
forty years of babies

and sores
long black hair
and marriage
collecting the monthly dole
this iron factory
the acrid fumes
the wasted creek
the forest for defecation
forty years beside Slovensky Raj
Slovakian Paradise
ten kilometres from
the highest castle
ten more from the highest church
these virgin people
carrying babies on their backs
hearts in their hands
and hopes
forty years of home

## Long Eyes

these women with their long eyes
scratching in dark rippled soil
for shards of light
in a late afternoon's
dropping sun
have come to their doorways
holding babies
babies
wrapped in the future
with leaves from the past
and held by strong thin fingers
thrust forward
like barter
all what they have
all what they are
a breath of certainty
amongst the boarded hovels
crouched about the low heat
the thrashing dullness
of embered waiting
these Roma women
with their persistent centuries
and long, long eyes

## Truncheons

sounds echoing from walls
armor glistening
this is the cadence of teeth
black as drained blood
these are police
no eyes
no faces
incisors hidden

body armor
carapace of attack
boots
crunching asphalt
protecting society
us
our freedom

truncheons
crashing against shields
again
again
again
in unison
marching
hundreds of black helmets
round worlds of obedience

thick muscle

## The Wrong Side

what exactly happened with Nagasaki

is it true that 50,000 were killed
by one bomb
40,000 died later
and there was radiation
and birth defects for years

there must have been quite a number of children
old people
I wonder what that was like
a world exploding
all the fire
the black rain

in one great detonation
a vanishing
of memories
songs
laughter
blood

all so immense
that no words
could ever fit the truth
more immense than any deed
of Attila
Genghis Khan
or other ruthless barbarism

more in the nature
of Pol Pot
Stalin
Hitler
the Hutu butchery of Tutsis

being on the wrong side

## Crossing Paths

from time to time
we cross paths with the dead
sighing so softly
we almost miss the melody
their cold skin
rises against our busy mouths
jabbering about deals
the dust on the road
the dead know us
and we them

oh it can be hard to look
hard to stop
breathe in slowly
let the footsteps get near
touch little fingers
the tiny cuticles of readiness
this is the pitter patter
of millions of raindrops
passing into the soil
humming their lullaby

these are the unanswerable koans
of back alley syllables
the greedy gestures of entitlement

only the rich are cheated of stillness

their money mattressed
like weevils in the flour
their mirrors pasted with fake roses
angst ennui and projects all in competition
for blood

while the poor
cheapen themselves hoping to measure
through the eye of that needle
to prick the promised heaven

the rat's feet
the scratching of nooses
the windy remorse
for all those villages
we've allowed to burn

## Angels

these days it's safe to say that angels don't exist
unless you've
never heard of Darfur
Somalia
Uganda
the downtown eastside of Vancouver
Virginia Tech
orphanages in China
the Roma of Slovakia
Tutsis
Sierra Leone
the Lord's Resistance Army
Iraq
the Taliban
Guantanamo Bay
Omar Khadr
suicide bombings
Robert Mugabe
Dick Cheney
street kids in Brazil
divorce laws in the Middle East
or Kosovo
unless they're
lazy
don't keep up with world affairs
on contract exclusively to Oprah
or are working both sides of the table

## The Ones on the Bottom

first a truck-load of pigs passes
as we sit at an outside table
sipping jasmine tea and
waiting for our overnight sleeper bus
to Guangzhou

the pigs all pink and squeezed
into tube-like woven baskets
stacked eight to ten deep
probably 200 of them in the back of that truck
the ones on the bottom
barely breathing from the weight

pork is a favourite
here in southern China
so is duck
all glistening golden brown
basted in its own juice

and before long a bus passes
laden with scores of ducks
half wedged in and tied to the roof
the other half tied to the back of the bus
most of them having given up the fight
and dangling
their heads tossing limply
the others still alert and struggling
not to give into panic

hoping I guess
that this is just some miserably dark nightmare

that before long
they'll return to their pens
by the Li River
and in the next dawn
once again waddle joyfully
down to the water
and paddle aimlessly
with the current

## Market Day

I am sitting on a bench
alone in a barber shop
the barber is playing his erhu for me
notes slide from the bow
as his wrists bleed memory
and my heart does move

today is market day in Yangshuo
the alleys are lined with bicycles
people have come in for the movies
and to sell
or buy

their patches of produce
face each other in a din of double rows
for almost a kilometer
peanuts heaped in white woven plastic sacks
mounds of amber tobacco
neat circles of white roots
or green bok choy
carrots
dried chillies
melon seeds
and white dumplings steaming
in the crisp morning air

to one side
are four men with propane torches
the awful sounds of the blue flame

they patiently work the flesh
lifting and turning
the faces of the pigs

and the puppies
to rid them of softness
leave only a stark grimace
and their pale limp bodies
to stiffen
amidst the mist
of their entrails

## Gibbon

stretch out your hands
past the moaning of the wind
as it rushes
over the folded lips of limestone
all pouty and waxen
in a timeless sulk
the monstrous karst monoliths
burnished in amber
jagged in cream and dusk

stretch out into the creeping
green moisture of a million branches
and leaves
and vines
of rain forest
poking triumphantly from every crevice and fissure
demanding more than life
root systems greater than imagination
gripping   limning   winding so intricately
they might belong to the rock
as veins

and there is the sound
of the gibbons' song

chorusing down from the misty slopes
a match for the sunrise

their dark faces rimmed
by immaculate fur
and long handsome limbs
that find safety in any perch

that can stretch out long
black fingers
to me
when I see them chained
four feet from a post
to amuse the customers

and a silent mouth
that has no song

## Franklin Feeds Babies

Franklin
feeds babies
through tubes
into their
tiny
noses
he wants to see
them smile

such a big man

he's
watched child soldiers
sleeping in Uganda
outside his hospital
heard them
scream
in the night
machetes whirling so fast
in the blinks of their eyes
watched fields of corn
turn to dust
amongst the empty words
and questions
no one answers

Franklin
cradles his memories
in their delicate graves
and drops petals
of hibiscus
into the rushing rivulets
of the rains

## Ode to Flies

what words would fit
for the flies
that alight on bodies
their dull black
and luminescence
doing their steady solemn study
on the dead

the old leper
baking two days in the Nagpur sun
dusty cotton     brown as the lane

the flies texturing his presence

the other man cloaked in his wheelchair
after Katrina in New Orleans
days with no attention

from any of us

the gracious flies filled
with recognition and acceptance

no violins for these funerals
no flowers from the guests

but the welcoming drone
of hundreds of tiny wings

## Young Teen on the Metro

the soft skin of a child
in her torn jeans
and wide silver belt

short snippy sentences
no texture of thought
all in the softness

eyes open

for all to see

new skin

what every woman wants
what every man wants

## Picture of Adam

you're told to smile
and you do
because they want it
expect it

and you like to smile

but your bones are broken

your eyes are ready to laugh
your little hands ready to stretch out
your chest ready to heave with laughter

but their fingers have gone to your throat
bruises map the softness of your five year old back

and no one wants to hear about it
know about it

so you smile

## Personal

when a man is beaten to death

the blood warm on fingers

wet on the boot
with the heavy impact of flesh

over and over

flesh so familiar

the nose losing shape

eyes swelling and ceasing to exist

jaw separating to shards
with no memory of voice

ribs snapping
imploding like hollow drum beats

body just a corridor for pain

when you beat a man to death
far past silence
is it personal
like the meeting of lips
the whispers you first heard
when you were born

## Gerwin

winding my way
past the vomit and glass
the Balmoral's orange lights
winking
sex inside
sex inside
Vancouver's chill
has frost in the air
crystals creeping into the pores
of the sidewalk
rubbies and whores
jerky statues of memory
wraith my path
and a voice lunges out

*hey . . .*
*hey!*

my eyes speed ahead
I haven't heard a sound

*hey . . . . hey*
*wait!*

the words stretching for my back
trying to become smaller
I don't have any change
no smokes
don't want a bag
don't want to look

*hey*
*hey . . . . Mr. White!*

what?

the street knows my name?

a black overcoat catches up to me
*Mr. White*

I know this person
it's Samuel Gerwin
played basketball for me in grade 12
a sloppy, wild player
with rare moments of penetration
and hot hands
he always wanted more time on the floor
the handsomest guy in the school
hair a black sheen
eyes bright as edges
fine smooth skin
the sight of him could take your breath away
but he spoke with a tic
mouth yawning mechanically
at the start of each sentence

his hand is still warm
tells me he's well
pleased to see me after all these years
but has to stop the smack
got stabbed in the side
a while back
doesn't ask for money
asks about my kids
what I'm doing
if I still coach ball

where I live
why I'm in Vancouver
then we part

it was good to see him again
a good fellow
blocks later I'm still tickled
how I thought the voice
was some rubbie
or junkie

and it was
only Gerwin

## Swallows

there are times when I can't remember
what it's like to breathe
in the moment
when an eclipse of the moon
is only ink on a page
umbra giving way to penumbra

a dark glow on the river shore

the swallows all frightened
and gone their beaks dripping
feathers arced against the cold
and me
wishing to be naked on the stones

but when I touch my skin
bare as the stones
it has no feeling
it can't lift me high
over the clay banks
like the birds
long from their homes
pocked in those layers just across from me

how freely they fly
hardly needing their wings

## Burqas

my students asked me what a burqa is
they're pants slung low
cleft between two white buttocks
smiling
asked what landmines were all about
why anyone made them in the first place
is it *Kabool*
or *Kawble*
the boys gathered round to watch the fighting on YouTube
the *ratatattat* into our enemies
running from one clay wall to another
just like in their favorite video game
no curiosity about how warm blood feels when it gushes

our enemies
look so odd
their faces rugged
syllables so much of a mouthful
cannot have any actual meaning
what are they saying?
strange clothes
even their bread is flat

our enemies
are bad people
in the hallways
the janitor checks for lunch bags thrown away full
complains with the teachers about the bad language
*fuckin A ..........fucking rights*

## Atrocities

how many words should be written
about a death
until that death
has justice

until we know it

what words
ones that can bleed
or moan
or shriek in agony

words that form the texture
of our baby
or mother
pleading for help
over and over

that etch meaning
like the sharp blade
lovers use
to dig time into the skin of a tree

how many
to put the silent grip of our fingers
on the small curve
of a trigger

how many words
to create even
a momentary whisper
that will stop us
from turning to the next page

## Not Gunshots

pretty days
with clothes on the line
thin yellow shirts
pillow slips
cotton socks
the sun warm
above the frayed grass
struggling against the dust
a breeze bringing a scent
of tiny hazel blossoms
like memories of first love
we all ask
for only pretty days
not gunshots
not footsteps
not questions
that hurt to answer

## Sentenced

we execute people
the same skin
warm to the touch
wrinkled in age
or smooth
and bearing little clear beads
of sweat
the same skin
warm to the lips
texture of mountain ranges
cool winding creeks
rich furrows in cropland
the palm of a hand
a covering of blood
a grey wren
pecking at winter berries
a deer
still as a tree and staring
at a strange movement
we execute
in the name of Jesus
or Allah
with nails
and verdicts
and scalding values
that power lets us have
we execute
with our prayers
and our silence

## While You Sleep

your knives
have the stain of old men
your teeth the cords of moments
reduced only by the light
fall of rain
as autumn chimes another dying
and you
you have forgotten how to breathe
hair as strewn
as lost sighs

I watched you asleep
on a path by the great river
horses alone in the sun
grazing by your feet
you were not angry then

your face chipped from the wind
your dreams hissing colour
ah, how you
moved
moved in the slow boughs
of cedar

## The Bodies

who should wash the bodies

the snot from her nose streaked cheeks
squatting to pee in the gutter
outside the mercado the tang of hung goat flesh

Marcellino pressing off the dried kernels of corn
with his seventy year old thumbs
the mound slowly growing larger
the blisters on my thumbs

sisters waking arm in arm
along the narrow strip of gray beach
burlap in hand to sieve the krill
from the surf
their hands on mine to their home on stilts
the white cake of cooked krill
in my mouth
the cold cooked platano in my mouth
it's what they have

the high hill
hot in the sun
behind the village
hot in the sun
the shrine on top
the voices of little girls
chorusing over and again
in rain songs
their eyes bobbing and lifting like human stars
with the lilt
the sea so warm
no fish

the river behind the village
flaunting the rain
from hundreds of miles distant
the river brown and fast
the house on stilts
scorpions skittering
bumping wickedly amongst tiny pebbles

Angelo on his knees
rubber tire pads
walking on his knees
his black face clean and pure
as slick as the sun
ready to shine my shoes
spitting
snuffling his nose
scratching his ear
and staring at me

that kid maybe eight
loping behind my bus laughing
calling at me about pesos
*hey mister!*
*hey mister!*
and when the bus halts
for more passengers to wedge inside
the teenage face that suddenly hovers
outside my open window only inches from my eyes
staring and grinning in silence
until the bus coughs back into gear

who should wash these bodies
when we're finished with them

## Bell Woman

1.
bell woman's hair strings grey
squeezing out more than the black
more than monthly blood

desperate steps along the pockmarked pavement
bell calling
steady relentless obsession
paraded
fingering the growling drunks
later
fingering their hair
for strands of her father

she pauses to examine
the great cold plate window
of THE ONLY SEAFOOD
wincing through the mirror shell
to a clearer closeness
and peering in at soup eaters
searching for a known face
among the winos and wealthy
who risk fine food on the skids

and licks the glass a good-bye

bell woman you're on my lap
speaking of lost condoms
and poems you wrote to Buckingham Palace
*that place is full of cocksuckers*
you're on my lap

2.
we drove you to the hospital
the quiet of the back seat
folded us limp to become an empty car
driving on its own to Emergency
frail I felt the warm bones
in your body struggling
beneath hungered skin
the normal brown turned to pale
scaring even the purple mascara
your face was already a mask without that

I felt your heart still alive
bundled with your body
squirming against my arms
and steps to the elevator
the clean floors
you hollered at the nurses
called them cunts
and sent howling *no no no's*
trailing down the long colour-coded hallways
the elevator doors
closed like hands over your mouth
and you draped into me
pee warmed in wetness on my leg
signing your signature on the admittance form
fourth floor

ah bell woman
are the sounds
to warn us
or to call us

## In Our Time

the old
are left
to fend for themselves
as though they were never us

care homes cut and dried
propped so proper
a nurse
a meal
a game
of bingo
someone's uncle
mother
walking the metronome plod
into doors that don't open
stairs that go only to a different set
of walls
TV's and hymns on Sunday
a Mormon spreading the good word

a code to get out
for those on duty

the relatives
with their empty
plastic bowls
at 7 P.M. after the special Easter dinner
with their fond memories
of Ed
of Bessie
names in big black letters
temporarily assigned to pale pine doors

the quiet in the halls
a voice from room number 22
pleading for a glass of water
*please!*
*please!*

and the smiles
from the large black and whites
on the wall in the foyer
a young woman in her wedding dress
eyes shyly downward
a large hand tender on hers
thick chested husband
staring expectantly outward
two others sharing a crosscut saw
well into a stout cord of fir
a thin blond boy
in ball cap and bare knees
girl in an army uniform
pointing to a barracks
her laughter
all but cracking the gloss

## A Common Moon

it's a long way from Haditha to Darfur

a thousand burqas away

yet desert to desert
the deep haze of dry death
drives

because it can

power
power speaks
with the deliberation
of scimitars and AK47's
the deliberation of lies
and pretence

duller than beasts
not deranged
but arrogantly limited
unable to grasp the concept of decency
they rode their armored chargers

alone
huddled together for the
pitiable notion of comfort
the children hid their eyes
from their mothers' despair

held each other until
the blood loosened their grip
slumped silent in heaps of warmth

the Janjaweed locked arms with the marines
and raised their throats to the moon

## Translucence

every night
a man comes down from the ridge
winding through the dying pines
and crashing across the creek

to ask about my father
who has died years ago

he refuses to accept this answer
and sampling handfuls of raspberries
says he'll wait

I'm used to him
and he to me

so even though I never offer him
a cup of tea
he waits patiently while I drink mine
and when I yawn and stretch out for bed
he lies down beside me and watches

when it's all dark
and I'm breathing
the slow wandering breath before sleep
I know he's awake
and if there's a bit of moon
he'll tell me I'm like marble or alabaster
all translucent and smooth
that my face is small and soft
hair as blonde as light

and as I fade to sleep
just before he leaves
I can hear him whisper
my name

## Beautiful Mornings and Dead Bears

beautiful mornings
push silence further
and even the grey pavement
asks forgiveness
as those four rigid legs
prod into the air
the soft black fur
thickening for the winter

a young bear
the kind that makes you stop
and stare

makes you want to reach out
as though the one you used to hold
had remembered your name
tried to find you again
but got lost looking up at the stars

saw those calling its name
and tried to go there instead
the thick pads of its feet
etched in lines of star light
where spirit passed to sky

## Taliban #2

our government does not negotiate
with terrorists
men with beards
and rifles
grenades
hand held rocket launchers
men who kidnap
and behead
as though the blood that flows is different from theirs
men who believe in paradise
dream of virgins
men who dominate women
as though women
had blood different from theirs
men who hide in the mountains
disguised as dust
erupt on the sides of roads
with steel destroying audacity

our government
hates these evil doers
their swarthy cowardice
wants us to sign up
and sign on to get them
make the world free again
our government is righteous
never lies
and protects us from ourselves

our government thanks God
we are the land of plenty
and fairness
pure water
and freedom
to buy and sell
as we please

## Afternoon on the Reserve

sometimes
I want to
cry with you
on the hillside
after three
bottles of white wine
crash through
the bushes
and your mind is
running
naked after deer
and yelling louder
as you trip
in one careless
leap

the deer is gone
and there you lie
alone with beating
moments from the
drums below
breathing harshly
as the sky waits quietly
for the clouds to move
over your face

## Coolness of Air

what is your relationship
with the coolness of air

how does it compare
to the moon
so full and silver
with finger ridges
it has taste

to the small
bird
silent in grey fluffed feathers
and death
as it lies in the hand
all still
to a morning of
bright birches in a sunshaft
on the hillside
their bark so white
so white

## She has Become

an *x*

each red line inches long

cut
deeply
into her leg
just above the ankle

a cutter
we call her
mesmerized by the slices in her flesh
the outer routes of blood
how exposed
she has become

her little girl fingers dipped so deeply
in this soundless artistry
of pain

how fierce
she has become

## THE HIGH SEASON

the spider feet
spider hands
fold around the grey ridges
and he moves his body
into a crouch
half way up the fifty foot palm

how long has it taken since
its first green shoots poked
from a hard brown husk in this sand
who was alive then
was there a fear about ozone thickness
in this tropical sky
were there talking movies yet
ah but why does it matter

he's at the top now and the
great green fronds are falling
from his sharp tooth of an axe
each whack severs the life up there
clumps of green bowling ball coconuts
seed clusters
and the great fronds
that give this rustic resort its shade
and its name - Palm Point

the tourists sit at morning coffee
and stare
in silence
as the suddenness of the axe thuds
the whooshing of the
falling branches
replaces the awe for the cutter's

spidering climb
ten feet from the top
a yellow arc is hacked
from the hard grey flesh of the trunk
to keep that last stretch of
the palm's triumph
from accidentally smashing down amongst the coffee cups

then the deadly growl of
a Stihl 070
its twentieth century four foot blade
melting through the prehistoric base

and now it's all manageable
in bucked up chunks
and one sad stump

next week the new cement
of the restaurant extension
will be setting
ready for the high season

## Dancing Bears

on the road to Fatepur Sikri
they lead fluffy black bears
by the nose
their teeth all muzzled
and claws long gone
they lead them along
the roadside
waiting to sidle out into the lane
and entice a tourist car to stop
then for the right fee
a few rupees
the bear will dance
its shaggy black coat
looming high
staggering about the road
and the people
will laugh to see such a sight
while the owner watches
with his long hard cane lying close at hand

## Morgaine Left the Hospital

and with her hands
cradled the blood
and tiny clear fingers
of her embryo

bent to kiss at lips
with broken tenderness

the fluttering of heartbeats
exhilarated at almost being born
has stopped
and in silent blood
smoothes desperately past
her palms
desperately searching
for soil or sea

with her moaning

## Burial

the time in mid afternoon
when autumn's October air
is especially sharp
alder leaves burned past yellow
and a thin breeze
pulls you into memories
we were walking away from town
our feet sweeping through dried grass
on the narrow trail
a faint ribbon along the hummock
guarding the railway tracks

in the field across from us
stark apple trees clung to the sky
some still swollen with fat globes of red
in this good year for fruit
and a farm woman all alone
plucked at the last of the pears

above us
winter wrens perched silently
in the fading season

I wondered if Neil felt much pain
as he lay dying
earlier that day at one A.M.
if when the knife drove deep
into his chest
his heart was surprised
the blood warm and loud
on his hands
as he clutched at his helplessness
if he thought about his baby son

with the dark brown curls
or his own mother
how she had held him
not all that long ago
at 22 it's so easy
to look both ways

and as the path dipped
closer to the tracks below us
we noticed silver fur
rolled long and still
over the flattened grass
a dog
half husky maybe half shepherd
as calm and natural there in death
as the wrens we passed
or the snowberry bushes
all huddled in a wait for winter

and when the dog had neared
this place by the tracks
was it to find his spot to die
sensing the end of moments
or was it a painful stagger
reeling from some farmer's poison
his black lips
pulled in faint grimace
or in welcome

yet either way
his body now offered to us
what were we to do
no one to tell
no one to care
or dig a grave

but us
and later
how easily
the soil parted
for the shovel

## Ice Portraits

like the morning designs
intricate jagged corona of crystals
within the fragile boundary
of each
small puddle
these momentary haloes
casting the spirit
of the water

when my mother was dying
of cancer
long weeks short months
could no longer move
in the bed
her personality
still gathered
within the stretched tight skin
clinging to her assemblage of bones

when my mother was dying
she had long stopped seeing visitors
each day
filled with other visions
just a waiting number
spoke only in response
focussed inward
we brushed her thin red hair

when my mother was dying
those years ago
she cursed herself
for crying
wanting it to be different

said she
hadn't wanted
to feel sorry for herself
the sores on her hips from
the relentless wave of the bed
edging her with pain
her mind wandered
the moist raw cavity
where her breast
had become cancer
was no longer
any part of her

when my mother was dying
and hadn't eaten
for days
acid burning inside
with any hard swallow
we bowed our heads
crushed
watermelon flesh
spooned her the juice
sip
by
sip

## The Score

in this time of global warming
words are insufficient
the immensity
we live in
so vastly beyond us
we who puff our chests out
wax about great achievements
as though we understand great
immerse ourselves in small-mindedness
the score of a game
who has dumped who
celebrity and cars
lawns
sharia law
papal decrees
tuxedos and costumes for every occasion
politics
professional wrestling
degrees and careers
memorized scriptures
sales and discounts

we are capable of more

we are the only species
that wonders
invents
cries for others who we don't even know

we are the only species
to conceive
respect
compassion

to contemplate
the future
our own death
the meaning of existence
where it all came from

yet
we bomb others
destroy our oceans and forests
stumble over what to do with the sewage and garbage we create
and sexualize our young

fortunately

we are also able to hope

## Taliban #3

everyone needs a Taliban
a bearded enemy
with glazed eyes
capable of the vilest deeds
capable of intruding
at any moment
to inflict pain
an enemy
to rail against
to spit at

to make us grateful for what we have
what we are given
add specialness to our own flag
beliefs
dreams

everyone needs a Taliban
even more than oil
or water
more than freedom
or rights
more than justice
or peace
definitely more than peace

a Taliban
to keep us alert
prepared
in fighting shape
focused on what matters
keep us together

everyone needs a Taliban

## Small Rivers

my mother and father are dead

the small river that flows through my property
cutting two pastures in half
barely covers the rounded brown stones
in the searing part of summer

the Salmon River it's called
has salmon come four hundred miles from the sea
to spawn
just a few each autumn
their reddish blue bodies
thrashing slowly     slowly
until they too die

the granular pebbles on certain parts
of the river floor
a nurturing place for the tiny fry
come spring

along the bank of the river
I once watched a dragonfly become luminescent
for its few weeks of light
the naiad slipped tentatively onto a flat black stone
waited in the sun
for its skin to leave
the bulging great eyes to appear
take in its new world above the water

I wondered how it might miss its years
in the stream
feasting on mosquito larvae
moving to and fro

with the current
would the unbelievable freedom of warm flight
be worth the count of days left in its life

my mother
left her husband when I was one
left his lost fury
to be far away and alone
with me

when my father died
he was shaking
in a hospital cot
never knowing
how a small river
can rise so high
it floods its banks
stretches far out into clover pastures

when my mother died
she talked about stars
and small craneflies
how if you look from just the right angle
you can see them kiss

## Autumn Oak

*you smell like chocolate cake*

*and you smell like eucalyptus* I reply
her arm wrapped beneath my back
we've just finished making love

in November she'll be 41
and as she stands naked in the doorway
scratching and fluffing up her hair
she tells me it's nutmeg brown

again on the bed
her fingers march softly along my side
*skin and bone*
*we're all skin and bone*
*just like in the museum*
she kisses me on the neck

and then in the kitchen making tea
still naked
she sings lightly
*O Canada glorious and free*
*we stand on guard for thee*
though I know she's the farthest thing
from a nationalist

we lay in the bed
sipping from the hot cups
and I watched her
looking out the window
at the brilliant orange
on the autumn oak

she really did
smell like eucalyptus

## Sitting with Swans

I'm cupped in the hands
of this October Sun
just at the northern point
of Strelecky Island
where the grassy shore
stretches slowly into the Vltava
only a few feet away
some standing
others floating like dreams
are the swans
so white
on the dark water
so white
nothing else matters

and then Bill Gates arrives
"how'd you like to work for me?"
he says
"I can guarantee you'll make a fortune."
he motioned for me to get up
and follow him
needless to say I was shocked
it was too good to be true
but there he was
grinning away in full confidence
waiting for me to move

if it wasn't for the swans
I'd have been right at his heels
"what's the matter?" he asked
pointing at the swans
all I could do was shrug
"those are just trash eating beggars,"
he sneered

"look how they follow the rowboats
hoping for scraps
they won't last long in this polluted river."
but I couldn't move
the swan closest to me
chattered at side feathers
then bowed and folded its
stunning long neck beneath
to tuck and prod the soft underdown
I watched as it lifted
a long black leg
flexing the webbing between its toes

"rich, you can be rich
buy your own swans
if you like them so much
drive a Porsche
two Porsches
and be known
even by the President."
he was exasperated with me

"but there's 44 of them
I counted," was all I could reply
in my defence

"you must be crazy
they're just birds, man
brains no bigger than peas
are you stoned?"

I watched how lightly on the water
they swept along
how elegant
their dark eyes curious

an intricate ballet
of stillness
Gates was angry now
and kicking at the ground
he turned away muttering
"fools, the world is full of them
the dumb ass doesn't
even want to work."
then I think he said
"good luck, buddy
you'll need it."

the swans paid no attention
to him or me
went about their business
of basking in that late afternoon sun
dipping beaks deep
for the tasty morsels
treading just above the river floor
he was long gone
when I realized my mistake
and wished I'd told him differently
that I was wrong
about there being 44
there were actually 45

## Conversations with Gulsara

when we face
the dying
eyes
reach into eyes

there are soft paths through the forest
thin brown pine needles and lacy fans of dried cedar
for our feet
new green
thrusting up through the dew
all around
the first fat bumblebees

we walk there

alone
whether we know it or not

the canopy of overhanging branches covering pieces of sky
as though what comes through
belongs to us

syllables as careful as lullabies
from feathers
each time we
utter
what we want
what we remember

## In the Pool

the old women
assemble themselves
for swimming
the pool
Sunday evening

their old flesh
oozing into the tepid water

an exhilaration familiar

eyes everywhere but to each other

the water
speaks memories
limbs
limbering for a night's affair
flesh
buoyant
titillatingly teasing
sumptuous
fingers tittering along the smooth bumps of the spine
breath along an ear
want
want
want
the quick taste of more
arching beneath these small small waves

the old women are
she
she groans
she undulates
grinds
they knows this water

remember
what it was

## Saskatoon 2002

I know a murderer
do you

he was the same height as me
we both had some acne

but I had friends
and he passed out alone in the toilet stall
while the rest of us
laughed and drank

he wasn't a bad shot
in the pool room

the hard cement walls so cold in summer
darkness all around
except for the clear light swathing the green felt
shining the colored balls bright and perfect

Grayson could shoot with the best

though the great welts that raised in instants
from each thud of Dunlop's fists
on his face
wrecked his game

the stories about his dad
and the war
the farm he built
from scratch
the crisp line of his suit
weren't the stories
that came from Grayson's lips

in 2002 he swam into death
with a young woman
he didn't even know
left her there
in pieces

his shackled legs
initialed with all the names
he knew

no one spoke to Grayson
no one listened to Grayson
the welts on his face
raising smiles
to ours

## Each New Year

we are men
of course
carved
into blocks of paper
as thin as new ice
hands to our mouths
grasping for the right words

and do we ever know?

we are left
with a dying bird at the roadside
fluttering
as we stare
at ourselves
the speed of our daily driving
negotiating
more than sharp corners
wondering only in times of crisis

left with age claiming time's due
hard skin becoming weaker though not always softer

are we all the hollow men?

which eyes frighten us the most?

families grow within our fences
and bodies shift and undulate
with intention of their own

we watch

a spectator
laughing on cue
weeping
when we can
and
waiting

## January 1 by the River

winter swans
white forms moving on the Shuswap River in the dusk
three skimming the surface
long necks stretched, wings powering them over the cold cur-
rent
and honking
swan voices
the other dozen looking upward

beyond in darkening distance
the violent sheer
of Enderby Cliffs
blocking where the January sun has dropped

we stand in silence
reaching from where we are on this bank
to be with the swans
paddle effortlessly
aside them
look into their dark eyes
have them know us
teach us
to fly

## Girl and Boy

do you remember the time we walked
through the springtime
to the old wooden water pipe
where the city gets its water
the new thick iron pipe had a leak
the spray shot thirty feet across the path
rainbows in the leaf sprinkled sky

we took our clothes off
imagined we were free in the twenties
when the wooden pipe must have leaked everywhere
the thimbleberry bushes
were rough on our thighs
bright red cup berries
sour and seedier than truth

you were afraid to go home
I laughed
as you sat by the turtle-shaped rock
and cradled your chin
wondering what you could say about your new blood

our fingers
all stained by the hundreds of thimbleberries
our bare backs stained deeper yet
by the fresh
sting
of the rainbow water

## Small Pebbles

the cots fabric the floor of this hostel for men
outside in the line a man reeked
I think I shit my pants he declared
the rest of us held our sides from the cold
happy to have a line to be in

tonight the snoring will give comfort
no wind
my shoes safe beneath the thin railing
that holds the thin mattress
my body
curled
like it has been
since I was a child

I have always been alone
a boy
crouched by strawberry plants
between the rows
wailing from a bee sting
the others
at the raspberry canes
further away

the men here
are all just like me
sweat memories rubbed in the creases
still about to laugh
at a fart whistling from the other side of the hall

there are so many eyes peeking into what is offered
so many silences
alongside the breathing
like the ripple hum of moving water over small pebbles

## Cruel Fates

what if the end is near
and Cuba survives
with its exploding cigars and bare shoulders
steaming azure lapping the sand
fuck
just imagine
all those years of stacking the deck
wanting to castrate Castro
the defiant etching of Che on all those bedroom walls
if Cuba survives
how fair will that be
we're the ones with the bomb
the beacon of freedom
and those
salsa bastards
play the fool with
nothing
now that'd be
a real downer

## Mystery

the salmon in the small river just fifty yards from my back door
have powered and gasped their way these seven hundred miles
from the Pacific
to the shallow of cold glass that I can wade across ankle deep
yet there they are
again
for the ten thousandth time
before the migration of men
before the heat from our poisons
the bite from our nets
brought such threat

what is it about innocence
about mystery
undeniable grandeur
that we so hate

## Don't Conplain Too Loudly

you never know who is listening
or worse
if no one is

after all
each of us is going to die

that moment
everything that was important
took sooooo much energy
took heart and soul

is gone

so when
you can find some birch trees
white bark as thin and perfect as love
leaves
green and frisky in the breeze
whisper
your name
your address
the time of your message
and what exactly
it is
that's
pissing you off

## Wreck Beach

we try to free ourselves

like leaves
before they die

sand trickles from my calves
naked men
and women
lie strewn on the beach
a species demanding to be noticed
the sun in every set of eyes
waves closing in

blackberries
grinning at us between
the thorns
the discrete sound of someone
pissing behind the bush
someone

there are at least three hundred steps to be trudged down
even more to get back up
most people never
actually come here
would rather imagine it
talk about it

at low tide
people skitter
to the surf
playing like children
whooping
as the wild cold water
clutches at balls
or breasts

back on the beach
the coarse warm sand
sticks
the toes
feel freer

## Sage

the plains Cree
burn the grey dried sage leaves
in the belly darkness of the sweat lodge
tiny sparkings on the red glow of the lava rocks
sucking in the flames
bodies tight together
huddled
facing the unbearable heat

the pulse
now emerged from the centre of the earth

the insides of the nostrils stick together
lungs sip frantically for air
the impulse to panic grows more urgent
as the prayers
linger

an etched rattle
older than panic
calls out courage

the heart releases and merges with the heat

the skin burning
slapping the back to bear the pain

then squeezing down onto the cedar boughs
face whispering to the soil beneath
the cool soil
the cool soil

the old man laughs

says *pretty hot eh?*
passes a water gourd
flicks a bit on the rocks
the steam for a micro second seeming a respite
then driving the heat deeper into every pore of bare flesh
suffocating
the sage
cleansing every memory

other than of being human

## The Gang Rapes of Lytton

catchy title too late to draw a crowd

the steep canyon walls of wind and whispers hurtling through the pines
below a vicious river open for bodies when they've had enough

we saw the faces

at school

days after

filled with age and distance
where once was only the vibrant expectation that each day was meant for them

filled with the signs of death

and

we the teachers

did nothing

our own dullness only excusable because we were that dull
our times that dull

we laughed and slapped shoulders with those boys and men who waited silently
in groups of darkness
outside the parties
waited like a deranged priesthood from centuries ago with gnarled fingers

and smug assuredness
to bury their poison so deeply inside their chosen ones
that the scent of their skin
would never leave

until some river called names to finish the job
some river offered to end the pain

## Hollow Boy

he was climbing the hill out of town
bare chested and bald, thin as the plastic of the bag he was lugging
was he 12 and on the run
I swung around at the bottom and went back to see him

*what's your story?* I asked
*where you going?*

*going to Nova Scotia*

*to see my dad*

*you alone?*

*no, I'm with my brother*
*he's up ahead*

eyes staring straight at me like an animal not knowing any better

*why aren't you with him?*

*we had a fight*
*so, I'm going on alone*

his skin a pale sheen
ribs and wild intention
away from what
6000 miles to what

*you hungry?*

*sort of*

not a stuffed man looking for purpose
not leaning together
but feet sore from being chased by rats
glass fragments hiding like gasps or wasps
ready to sting his unwanted future

he is our hollow boy
running
just out of sight

## We Pay

if the price of coffee goes up or down the price of gas goes up
or down we go up or down
but we pay
when the job disappears as though it never mattered what we
did what we felt all that time
we cry or go on our way
it must be nice to make 20 million a year like Alex Rodriguez
and the CEOs of main street
surreal but nice

the French take their bosses hostage

## Darkness

in the middle coach on the Montreal metro
123 heads are clamped with earphones
alone
as we enter Berri-Uqam
as we enter Sherbrooke
as we enter Laurier
this is a time of distance
the wide rubber wheels hard on the steel
as we enter Rosemont
no eye contact
which is no small feat
for 123 in one coach
the thrash of the train
an easel of permission
for this insular canvas of still people
bobbing and rolling ever so slightly
as we enter Beaubien
Jean Talon
no words for each other
for themselves
about intimacy or sadness
or how grapes grow wild and purple
and sweet
amongst the thinly furrowed oaks
on Mont Royal
as we enter Cremazie
if there are memories
or daydreams or ruminations
they are wearing all these bodies
naked in sameness
plugged out
and so alone they may as well have left
their ears where they came from

as we enter Sauve'
as we enter De La Concorde
and finally flush through the sliding doors
clatter onto the escalator
123 heads as one caterpillar
slowly inclining
toward the dark night ahead

## For Sale

it's hot on every street all over America
dogs chestnuts corn on the cob Corvettes and cleavage
and votes
buy em all now
that's what paychecks are for Johnny
cash em in and let the good times bleed or breed
marching bands will bear your instrument in times of need
you will be a tune
for the troops to come marching home
crisp as motherhood and virtual reality

get those fingers dancing
vote for America now
don't be a real nowhere man
a beetle to be stepped on
a vow to be forgotten in some lost Vegas chapel
be a *fucking* man
get down to the hardware store and buy some nails
triple your points
a vote for your congressman is a vote for jobs
apples in every basket
ice cream in 96 flavors
that even appeal to those terminally depressed
lick lick lickety split
call the farmers out of the dell
out of the chat rooms into the back rooms

make a deal with the boys
to buy Boredwalk
and paint new stars on the sidewalks
for all the newspapers that lied to the press
about who really killed JFK
who really turned in Nixon

who really taught Clinton the smoky facts of life
kept bumping Jerry on the head
and put our hearts in Viet Raq
yes I'll say it again
get your red hot votes
right here
while they last
and remember

if you don't play
you can't win

## Those Days of the Confident Glide

I only understood what time was after Jack Allan died

years before so clear
him angled with his cue across the green felt
of the number one pool table
light in a beautiful circle out of the dark cold walls
carving the green so brightly
that life was right there all of it the world solely the space on the
table between shots
Jack in his suit coat and cream coloured dress shirt
stretched in elegance aligning the shot
the perfect roundness of the white cue ball
the deeper red one asking to be struck
Jack's slow confident glide
the chalked tip of the cue
its long tapered varnish
ending with a precise *cluuuckk*
the white ball rolling true
and
*clak!*
the red turning over and over in inevitable conviction toward
the maw of the corner pocket
Jack holding the pose

all of us watching
the red

disappear

and then upright again Jack retrieving his fat cigar
and scanning the felt
to be sure the pink ball
was still the best colour to go after
ensuring the cue ball
was just where he had wanted to leave it

this was Friday night
in Armstrong
when I was fourteen
the four tables
decreasing in quality
the distance from the entrance
Jack Allan only ever at number one
his smart baritone
wink at the boys who watched
the crease in his fine trousers
what a shot he had

under the fedora
he was bald we knew
but the hat
the suspenders and the style
the style
plump with certainty
the way he held the cigar
how his shots fell
the line of his body
the smoothness from his shave
we watched this man
this certainty
studied the slightest movements and gestures
as one would Michelangelo

this was Armstrong
such a small town
three gas stations
and six churches
main street parallel with the tracks
a movie theatre with hair grease stains worn

in the back padded wall behind the last row
hardware store
a barber
drug store
shoestore
grand post office with a clock
and one other street cutting across
pillared bank
butcher shop
five and dime
clothing shop
a bowling alley below the grocery store
and Pete's Pool Hall
where hushes bought condoms
one at a time
and where the men came to play snooker
the boys came to watch

## Some Little Girls

the little girl in a daffodil dress
draws her oceans with the sparkly
tinkling glass shards
of a crack pipe
perched like a monument
as proud as sunlight
on the damp green
of this morning grass
her bare feet
open to the dewy texture
like a mouth
to the offerings of a mother bird

these are her days
alone with lovers hidden
in shadows
rock walls slanting against a prison entrance
teeth clenched

the thick grasp of sinews
wound like a wound
that never heals
tight to veins

this is her time
to gain inches
and
friendships
magic memories
of water
whispers
of love

## Troublemakers

I got pissed off today when the guy at the Ticketmaster kiosk
treated me dismissively
if I'd been braver meaner I'd have punched him in the mouth
just to wake him up
my wife doesn't like it when I talk violence it scares her
she looks at me nervously
yet I've seen her get the same way as me when someone really
crosses the line
but this isn't about me or her and our proclivities
it's about where people get the idea
that it's okay
to be an asshole to someone for no particular reason
like the city bus driver that sees you coming but closes the door
as shut as a slap
zips off with you chugging to a halt with your helplessness and
your leftness limp at your sides
like the lady at the counter in the government office that acts
like you are bothering her
that what you are asking or have filled out is some horrendous
affront and unacceptably inept
like the cop
who struts to your open window waggling his pretensions
prying them into your day the way the big kids did when they
were bored and you were only ten
when the whole purpose of the jobs these people have
is to serve the public

## Imagine

horses stretched out on the ground sound asleep look like
they're dead
big soft lips slightly apart
sprawled wherever in the middle of a sunny pasture

if allen ginsberg and john lennon were alive today
would they be texting on their cells
flushed with emoticons

## The High Country

a moose
cow or bull
alone in the high country
standing in the wet of a wide marsh
eating the sprigs and morsels that moose favor
the great thick head moving down to the damp pulling at the foliage
then upwards to chew
gaze about for movement ready to run but not worrying
because way out here there really is no threat for such a majesty such power
except a rifle
and the moose knows that by the time the rifle is spotted it's too late that running would only be for show so as not to give an impression that after all these millennia the moose couldn't recognize death when it arrives

## Like a Village

500 narwhals waiting to die
beneath the ice
their friendships
families
waiting to die
like a village in the Congo
only in Nunavut
it's 31 below
and the ice so thick
that hopes can't be felt

their great twisted tusks
and three thousand pounds of life
spiralling blue in the Arctic cold
a mile deep
than gasping for air to the surface light
when
there is
no
ice

what now is their song
a death song
that seeks the seam in the deepest current
to leave their spirit
they are ocean now
and the Inuit hunters
who wait for them to rise
ancient harpoons at shoulders
to carve the flesh
into shares across the north
the blood

that will turn the sea
these Inuit
know what it is to drown

they hear the songs
of the narwhal

## Sharing the Steam

they come in together every Thursday

their day at the pool

the one with the boyish frame
so much smaller than the big guy
him with his overflowing paunch
about forty maybe
round face
no expression

I could see him
alone in his apartment
drinking his fourth beer
watching
a porn movie
thinking
of the young life guard at the pool
the way her dark wine coloured swimsuit
skims her shape
how it stops right above the curve of her bum
to open the wide young flesh of her back
or
maybe smoking cigarette after cigarette
with his buddies
at a Texas hold'em table
inwardly cursing at the fall of cards
or maybe just a lonely bugger
stuck with limits
like the rest of us
as stuck as pitch

but the other guy
the other guy mostly rides

on the big guy's shoulder
as slight and hunched as a child
I thought he was a child
until I noticed the reclining hair
the pinched face of a thirty year old man
as he rode bundled
wound on the big guy
in the pool

as natural as love could ever be
the two of them

flowing together in the current circling the kids' pool
the broken guy's fingers covering his friend's mouth
as he held on
then as the current relaxed him
the fingers moving into the big guy's hair
examining the texture
the two of them going
round and round with the current

then later in the steam room
the slight guy flat and bent on the top tier
almost hidden in the steam
the heat caressing every grimace
every limitation

and it was hot

and the big guy
sitting nearby
head bowed in the privacy of the steam

## Ferlinghetti at Ninety

when I make my pilgrimage to the grave of Lawrence Ferlinghetti
I'll be sure to recite at least some words in Italian
some in French
mention his Aunt Emily

I'll scratch *endless life*
on the stone if it's not already there

I'll think about Patchen and Pound
Sandburg and Snyder
about all the footsteps he put on the pavement
to and from the rest of the world
to the rest of the world
about how he scrawled

*INDICT BUSH & CHENEY*

in bright black

for everyone to see every moment of every day hoping that their
crimes wouldn't be forgotten but knowing
they would

I'll bring a sprig of jasmine
from Golden Gate Park lay it atop the tomb
as though it was a garland for a fallen emperor

I'll think about how he decided to
stop having birthdays
because it meant the fun was bound to stop
sooner or later
how he winced at how stupid people could be when their brains
were filled with advertising and clamped by plastic tongs
threw his arms out to the gulls floating afar in the dark

waves of the Baja
brought them back in with hands filled with
glowing

how Lawrence loved to paint erections and open flow-
ers grappling on the backs of horses
at Hires Point
how he swam in long rivers
swam with Fidel and Che with Neruda and
long political porpoises the initials E R O S
gently etched
but indelibly etched on the soft knowing above their eyes

how his own eyes were blue long be-
fore blue was invented
how
his eyes
looked way past way past what everyone else

couldn't see

and I know for a fact that there will be small whispers coming
from the cypress needles far above
from the chestnut trees at Spoleto
from the broken chrysanthemum petals moving in the
wind at Nagasaki
from the wide fat oak leaves in the forests of Prague
from the slow setting dusk light of Big Sur
whispers.....

whispers.....

whispers.....

## Looking for Tracks

he walks slowly along the hard crust of this late March snow

we are in the mountains

the logging road is silent

to each side    all poking starkly up from their blanket of white
broken, red pines from the beetle kill
thick trunks of Douglas fir
and dark spruce
all aching from the long winter
whispering about the warm sun

he is a Sekani boy
a young father
he walks slowly in the blue sky
eyes scanning the undulations of snow
dipped trails angling up onto the road bank
and winding through the trees and underbrush
*a young cow moose*
he says
and *maybe*
*mountain lion tracks*
*farther back*

we are in the mountains
I am breathing in the warm sun
the glinting snow
the air
and silence

he scans for tracks
far behind me
the Sekani boy
the young father
his footsteps slow
on the hard crusted snow
eyes
studying
every marking

he was a child not so long ago
at his grandfather's knees
as they checked traps
for miles and miles
the bush
filled with the same peace
not like
houses
and their fists
or soft sticky hands
skittering silently slowly
along his thighs

tracks
in the mountains
meant possibilities

# Dogs

training
is everything
just enough time to bring the gums as far back from the teeth as possible

get the bark guaranteed to bite
and bite
and bite

in the Civil War and World War 1 and 2 they say
that many bullets went into the air or into the ground
they say that men didn't feel good about putting other men to death

so Viet Nam was the chance to do it
differently

get those dogs
to bite
every chance they got

snap the pussy right out of them
build that character
*DIS I PLIN*
I said *DIS I PLIN*
rip that doubt by the throat
squeeze the questions into man-sized *Yes Sirs*
draw those slanted eyes into gooks and VC and whatever name
brings out the right *sic 'em*
'cause no way it was gonna be the last war
this was training for the future

but just to be on the safe side
they dropped more bombs than all the sides together dropped in
World War 2
and scoured the jungle
with Agent Orange
napalm
and land mines

just goes to show you
some don't trust dogs
no matter how well they're trained

## Handrails

we're born in search of them
the strong braided ones alongside a perfect mother's cheek
soft hands
to cradle our own delicate skin
and leaping forward  to the moment we begin to live in our mind
it's the mirror that's our best friend
tells us how we'll be seen
and the gadgets
plugged in to keep the others out
plugged out to keep the others in
chatting should have several more t's
chattttttttting
safety in numbers
designer jeans become
lol
and (:
safe hand holds
like heaven
and the Democratic Party
or Father Benjamin
and the Green Party
or the
environment
it
self
MY VALUES ARE
and
according to Scientific American
on YOU Tube
Nietzsche said
my rights
I believe in justice and equality

I'm a history buff
go
Red Sox
as
though
it
all
matters

but it does
because everyone craves a handrail
who cares
what it's made out of
just like
mom
who cares

## Homeless

my son sleeps under a bridge

low over a small hidden creek
the ice still gripping smooth stones
along the edge

the water chirping as seriously as silence

his blankets all bundled and wadded
to cut against the cold
even out the juts of hard rock beneath

this is no faded grassy repose

this is the quick cold of winter
the greyness of banked stone

he wants no part of his past

wants only the sanctity
these moments
of water

## Something to Remember

it's probably a good thing I don't own a gun
a Glock 17 with
shells galore
*bang bang bang bang. . . .*
just like that

good thing
I'm not in the NRA

though I did some target shooting once
I could sight that Glock real well
several rounds
right into the target's head
from 15 metres
surprised the hell out of my buddy

good thing for all those assholes
that think they own the world
the ones at the beach that yell and swear
or let their dogs race all over
way past the signs that divide the dog area
no matter how many little kids are playing
or the guys with big muscles
push by you on the street so you're the one who has to step
aside

then again
maybe I'd get carried away
go even further
get in one of those dark moments
when a guy like George Bush
and Gitmo starts to get to me
feel overwhelmed by the way absurdity

and arrogance seems to rule
how gadgets
have replaced communion
how empty and primitive it's all become
cops lying and shooting
politicians lying and spending to kill
no one thinking deeply
no one questioning
no one in power caring if they do

maybe I'd get so fed up with it all seeming so hopeless
I'd just take that Glock
and find a way to change it all
just a bit
for a few minutes anyway

maybe put a bullet in the big shot's foot
just to get his attention
give him something
to remember

## Crows

there are lines that will never be written

trillions of them

that's the best reason
to enjoy the ones that are

each
is a new piece of the puzzle
of us

the thinking, pondering, reflecting, imagining animal

when Sandburg wrote about Chicago
he was in love
when Ferlinghetti wrote I Am Waiting
he was in love
when Yeats wrote about Innisfree
he too was in love

that's how it goes

when you're driving along a windy country road
and there a hundred yards in front
you see a crowd of black crows
they scatter
as you get near
beside your car
whizzing along
as though
it mattered
as much as
you wanted it to

beside your car
for that quick stupid second
you gave yourself to look
beside your stupid car
before your stupid eyes
is a mound
of broken red
deer
and
staring right into your stupid eyes
are the daring eyes of
an immense
eagle
talons sharp into the deer carcass
daring
you to even think about getting some of it

and thus
you too can be
in love

## When I was in Prison

not exactly
prison
a jail
in Mexico
I was young
felt immortal
*this is hilarious* I said to the Brit behind bars with me
*I'm Canadian* I thought
but inside I was uneasy
the Mexicans were scared
the Americans were scared
Susan was 8 months pregnant
we were all hungry
thin, milky soup that I wouldn't eat
and rice
we pooled money to send out for
tortillas frijoles
and
honey
the toilets had no doors
and a guard went along
liked to watch the American girls
there were 21 of us
all in one big cell
the Oaxaca 21
we made a pyramid of shoulders
to drape a cloth over the one bare light bulb high up that never
shut off
the cloth caught fire and broke the bulb
the guards were pissed
every so often a Mexican kid
was taken off for interrogation
came back crying

bruised
they never touched the gringos
except
I got lippy
in my turn
detective with a moustache
raised his fist in a fury
grabbed my beard and twisted it
I never cried

we had it easy

a week later
all got deported

not the Mexicans

## When Jerry was in Prison

everybody knew that it was Jerry
small town
armed robbery
19 year old
it had to be Jerry

running through the black
lanes of adrenaline
*I did it, I did it*
he'd tell me later
$284
and on the lam to Vancouver
the silver gun
in a dumpster

after three months
there was a trial
Jerry got a year

he had to wear orange
push through two lines of shoulders
to get to his bed
*never ever call someone a goof*
he'd tell me later
*don't whistle either*

at night Jerry slept lightly
a filed shank beneath his mattress
he'd seen a target get it in the dark
socks filled with bars of soap
*whap!*
*whap!*
*whap!*

he'd tell me later
the bruised face all purple and thick the next morning

those guys were really not so bad
if you weren't a bitch
or a rat
they were okay
from homes like Jerry's
fathers that liked their own brands of soap

## AND HE DIED TOO EASILY

the rough poles that joist above our heads
carry the mud and straw
that warm the winter
in these low homes
the women bent to the ankles
plucking at ancient songs
the dream of green corn
trembling in cool summer air
this is a desert
the blue of possibility
blocking the sun
blocking the early deaths
that sniff relentlessly
at every crevice
the brittle walls
flaking
lungs
coughing
coughing
he held my hand
so gently

## Man Walking Dog

in a great mist
bundled with wool against this March snow
the white furrows
crackle beneath boots
the pads of the dog's feet
warm and soft
as it gambols on the field
the hard earth
caught still in winter
doesn't yield to any pressure
but is lost so easily
in the mirth of the dog
the quiet choice of the man

## Chavez is Dead

his gold chains
and ruby stud
are in the ground
freedom and the courage pendant
embalmed
in sad exuberance
Chavez is dead
the soaring blare of his trumpet
ooze of viola tincture
lost now in the ever present
thrust of wind above trees
medicine is dead
land is dead
the fair shake is gone
for now
the prisons will open
and the glee of money
will return
to swill with oil
the tide
as it does
washing away the marks left on the sand
Chavez is dead
and sorrow
is alive
for now

## KINGFISHER

alone with van Gogh
in his gaze
those blue broken eyes
all about the blind fingertips of colour
where fields have no warriors
or banker's columns
but furrows of flowers
calling out to kingfishers
and the green tips of potatoes
and if there was a way
to touch the oils
the throbs of moment
as unmad as wind
grace his shoulders
as they moved the brush
hear the ooze of paint onto the palette
if there was a way
all the other ways
would not matter

## A Tighter Embrace

when the trees cast their leaves into red and brittle veins
that time in autumn when the brutal grey
of the statues to war
no longer chips the brightness of the sky
when lovers try harder to forget their hatreds
turn faces from the chill
ask of each other
a tighter embrace
and those who have died
sigh in the dreams of those
who carry them
this is the blessing of latitude
the carving of texture into the millions of moments
we are given
to breathe
placing grace before us
as softly
as the lone maple leaf that brushes
past our knee
to rest red on where we have been
why we want to sing
hear the sound of living voices
especially our own
how melody finds us in spite of ourselves
how the cedar
bends
and sifts the air
above the cold mountain brook
with the scented fingers
of recognition

## You and Me

we share the same moon
the same sun

one day yours
the next day mine

catch a breath
of the same wind

touch tea to my lips
as you tip the cup

we share the same tenderness
like lullabies in the night

## Acknowledgements

My gratitude to the following journals in Canada, U.S.A., New Zealand, and Austria for earlier publication of some of these poems: The Antigonish Review, Pottersfield Portfolio, Grain, Descant, CV2, Jones Avenue, Pearl, Whistling Shade, Read This, Windfall, The Southern Ocean Review, Poetry Salzburg Review.

Thank you to John Lent and Michael Donaldson for their guidance and humanity. Also thanks to Craig Warkentin, Virginia Dansereau, Allen Smith, Suzan Milburn, Vivian Plenge, Dennis Butler, and Ann Alma.

Thank you to Van Royko for the help imagining a cover for the book.